TOURING CARS

PRC

This edition first published in 1998 by
PRC Publishing Ltd,
Kiln House, 210 New Kings Road, London SW6 4NZ

© 1998 PRC Publishing Ltd

ISBN 1 85648 491 2

Printed and bound in Spain

Contents

Motor Racing and Touring Cars–an enduring passion

In 1886 Karl Benz was granted a patent for the Benz Patent *Motor Wagen* which first ran—falteringly—on the streets of Mannheim, Germany in June of that year. It lays claim to being the world's first proper car. Within a few months Gottlieb Daimler had successfully fitted one of his experimental petrol engines—the first practical internal combustion engine—into what he described as his 'horseless carriage'.

It did not take long for the new-fangled invention to spawn an all new sport—motorsport. In fact, the very first attempt at motor racing came just one year later in 1887 when the French magazine *Le Vélocipède* tried to organise a trial on the outskirts of Paris. Sadly, only a single car turned up which meant there wasn't much competition that day.

However, a more competitive event was arranged in 1894 by another French publication, *Le Petit Journal*. It attracted no fewer than 102 entries for its 79-mile trial between Paris and Rouen, though only 21 took the start. A de Dion steam-powered machine won the trial, averaging a heady 11.6mph.

The winning driver, the Marquis de Dion, wasn't even allowed to collect his prize as it was decreed that carrying two crewmen was in breach of the rules. The prize was divided instead between Peugeot and Panhard.

Despite the dispute, this first race grabbed the imagination of both the early motor manufacturers and the pioneer drivers. There was now no turning back. MotorSport had come of age.

Grand Prix, Grand Tourers and all sorts of other exotic branches of motor sport were developed during the 20th century. Generally, the cars destined for circuit racing were specially developed, tuned and designed for one purpose only—to win races. They didn't look anything like normal road cars and certainly did not perform like the asthmatic little saloons of the 1930s and 1940s.

It was not until the 1950s that saloon cars tended to be featured in serious circuit competition. The change came with the launch of new and far more powerful road cars such as the Jaguar Mark VII, a genuine 100mph car with handling and roadholding to match. Now it could no longer be said that road cars were too slow, too cumbersome and too unwieldy to provide any sort of a spectacle.

This was the moment that the motor manufacturers had been waiting for. They had always realised that saloon cars looking like the models gleaming in the showrooms offered a marketing potential of infinite value. Not only could they demonstrate the performance and potential of their cars, but if they could win races, they would at the same time demonstrate their technical superiority over their market rivals' models.

'Win on Saturday or Sunday, sell on Monday' summed up the thinking, which is why the manufacturers enthusiastically supported events such as the *Daily Express* Production Saloon Car race held during the 1952 Silverstone Formula One meeting and in the following years the *Daily Express*

International events which saw the likes of Stirling Moss showing the capabilities of the Jaguar Mark VII.

Though these one-off events attracted large crowds and were very popular with drivers and manufacturers, it was not until 1958 that the first British national saloon car race series started. It was the brainchild of Ken Gregory, best known as the manager of the incomparable Stirling Moss. He had seen the growing popularity of saloon car racing during the 1950s and wanted to provide a forum for Britain's war-ravaged motor industry to display the prowess of their latest cars.

His idea was for a national race series for current production cars, with four individual classes to allow cars with different engine sizes to compete together. Initially, the classes were for engines up to 1,200cc, 1,201-1,600cc, 1,601-2,700cc and 2,701cc and above.

In the event, the first championship could not have produced a better result. Class winners Tommy Sopwith in a Jaguar 3.4 and Jack Sears in an Austin A105 Westminster tied for the inaugural champion's garland. Instead of sharing the prize, it was decided to hold a tie-breaker in which the two drivers drove identical Riley 1.5 cars in a challenge event at Brands Hatch. Sopwith won the first five-lap race by 2.2 seconds. The two then swapped cars and set off again for a second race which Sears won by 3.8 seconds and was therefore declared the winner.

The following year, the title was clinched by Jeff Uren in a Ford Zephyr, and in 1960 it was Doc Shepherd in an Austin A40 who won the overall trophy.

Above:
Gordon Spice won the 3,000cc class five years in a row from 1976 to 1980 in his Ford Capri

Below:
The Triumph Dolomite Sprints were fast and evil-handling but Andy Rouse drove one to become BTCC Champion in 1975

Above: Minis could never hope to win outright but by clocking up numerous class wins Richard Longman won the Championship in 1978 and 1979

An important move came in 1960 when the British Racing & Sports Car Club (BRSCC), the organisers of the Touring Car Championship, decided to adopt the FIA's regulations for European Touring Car Races. It still meant that only series production cars were eligible, but it allowed more technical development than had previously been permitted.

Manufacturers had to provide proof of the number of production cars actually produced, and they also had to make available for sale to the general public any engine or bodywork modifications that they made for their race touring cars.

Up to this time, though they had always been pipped at the post by smaller-engined cars for the overall title, it was the big Jaguars which had won the majority of races outright and which had consistently won the 2,701cc and above class. F1 aces Bruce McLaren, John Surtees and Graham Hill all competed in the big cats and even Colin Chapman, boss of Lotus, found time to compete in 1960 with Roy Salvatori in Mark II Jaguars.

Yet the Jaguars were already beginning to be outclassed by new American entries—such

as Dan Gurney's Chevrolet Impala—which produced massive horsepower and immense top speeds on the straights. The Jaguars tended to catch up under braking for corners, but only to see the American V8s disappear into the distance once more.

Yet with the new regulations, it was not to be this brute force that would win the championship outright; nimble handling proved itself the premium characteristic.

In both 1961 and 1962 the overall titles were taken by Minis, driven by John Whitmore and John Love respectively. In many ways this provided a great boost for the British Touring Car Championship (BTCC). The little Minis with their giant-killing exploits proved extremely popular with the crowds as they swarmed all over their much larger competitors, taking class win after class win in the series.

In the next couple of years, the championship was dominated by the unlikely combination of more massive American V8s— notably Ford Mustangs, Galaxies, and Falcons, and Chevrolet Camaros—and a newcomer to the touring car scene, the Ford Lotus Cortina.

Ford in Britain wanted to bring even closer the relationships between the ordinary family saloon and the cars that swept to victory on the racetracks, and so the company commissioned Lotus to turn the humble Cortina into a winner. Lotus put a new twin-cam cylinder head onto Ford's 1.5-litre four-pot unit, rebuilt the suspension with coil springs in place of leaf springs and painted the cars a memorable two-tone colour.

Although Jack Sears was overall winner again in 1963, it was none other than Jim Clark in a Lotus Cortina who clinched the honours in 1964—the first and only time that the Formula One World Champion was also British Touring Car Champion. In fact, Jim Clark took 15 class wins and eight outright victories in four years of Lotus Cortina racing.

Victory went to Roy Pierpoint's Ford Mustang in 1965 and to John Fitzpatrick's Ford Anglia in 1966. 1967 and 1968 belonged to Frank Gardiner who was champion first in a Ford Falcon and then in a Ford Lotus Cortina. He would win the touring car championship for a third time in 1973, driving a Chevrolet Camaro, but in the meantime yet more rule changes, which effectively banished the increasingly competitive Porsche 911's and other sports cars from touring car races, paved the way for small-engined cars to come once again to the fore.

Alec Poole came out on top in 1969 and the next three consecutive seasons were dominated by Bill McGovern in his 1.0-litre Sunbeam Imp.

Frank Gardiners' third championship in 1973 in his Chevrolet Camaro was to be the swansong of the big American V8s which were soon to be outlawed by yet more rule changes.

It was Bernard Unett's Hillman Avenger that was victorious in 1974 and Andy Rouse's Triumph Dolomite Sprint in 1975—the first of four championships that Rouse was to win in a long and distinguished touring cars career.

For the next four years, it was the sub-1,300cc class that was destined to provide the overall championship leaders. Bernard Unett won twice more, in 1976 and 1977, in a Chrysler Avenger GT and then Richard Longman in his Mini 1275GT took top honours in both 1978 and 1979.

Although small-engined cars were consistently taking the overall title, the one to beat to the chequered flag was the Ford Capri. Once the big American V8's were off the scene, it was the 3.0-litre Capris that emerged as the front running models, clinching numerous class wins in the late 1970s. Most successful Capri driver was Gordon Spice who won the 3,000cc class title five years in a row between 1976 and 1980.

The Japanese started to take a serious interest in the touring car championship in the 1980s, and it was the radical rotary-engined Mazda RX-7 that provided Win Percy with the first and second of three successive overall

Above: Win Percy led the field in his rotary-powered Mazda RX7, clinching the championship in both 1980 and 1981 before switching to a Toyota Celica and winning again in 1982

titles. His third, in 1982, came at the wheel of another Japanese make, the Toyota Celica.

Win Percy's three in a row titles were followed by three in a row for Andy Rouse. In 1983 it was with an Alfa Romeo GTV6 that he took the title in contentious circumstances; the top three drivers had all competed in 3.5-litre Rover Vitesses but under the FIA's revised Group A rules, all were excluded, a move which promoted Rouse in his 2.5-litre class GTV6 to outright champion.

By the following year, eligibility disputes had been sorted out and it was ironically at the wheel of the Rover Vitesse that Rouse took the title again in 1984. The next year, in 1985, Rouse won nine out of the 11 rounds in his Ford Sierra Cosworth Turbo which heralded a new era in the BTCC—that of the turbo.

Rouse remained a front runner in 1986, actually winning six rounds, though it was to be Chris Hodgetts in his fast and ultra-reliable Toyota Corolla who would take the title in both 1986 and 1987.

By 1988, touring cars were drifting further and further away from standard saloon cars. Two-seater sports cars were still banned, but the manufacturers were now creating saloons specifically for racing. Ford's Sierra RS500 Turbo and BMW's M3 were classic examples

of this new genre: cars designed and built with the racetrack in mind and which were offered for sale to the general public in just enough numbers to ensure homologation—admission into the BTCC races.

The 1988 season saw Rouse achieve nine outright victories in his Sierra RS500, but Frank Sytner in his BMW M3 did even better and his 11 class wins were enough to give BMW its first ever touring car championship title.

The all-new Astra GTE 16V took John Cleland to the title in 1989 and in 1990—the last year in which touring cars raced in classes according to their engine capacity—Rob Gravett took the overall title in his Ford Sierra Cosworth RS500, the car that had dominated the top class for the previous three years.

For 1991, all BTCC entries had to be 2.0-litre cars using unleaded fuel. Vauxhall, which had just launched the Cavalier, was one of the leaders that year but in the end it was Will Hoy in a BMW M3 who took the top honours. The two following years, BMW again dominated with first Will Hoy in a BMW 318is and then Jo Winkelhock in a BMW 318i taking the title.

The new 2.0-litre formula resulted in greater manufacturer interest than ever in the BTTC with Mitsubishi, Nissan, Toyota, BMW, Ford and Vauxhall all keen rivals on the track. It also resulted in closer and better racing, and therefore even larger crowds at BTCC meetings.

In previous years the championship had often seen runaway winners, but no longer. Competition was so intense and, under the new 2.0-litre formula, performance was now so similar, that no one car could totally dominate the field. In fact, during the 1991 season, four drivers—Will Hoy in a BMW M3, Steve Soper in another BMW M3, Andy Rouse in a Toyota Carina and John Cleland in a Vauxhall Cavalier—each won three times, and Hoy only grabbed the title in the final race by picking up points for a fifth-place finish.

1992 proved yet another turning point for the BTCC as TOCA Ltd took over organisation and promotion of the championship. TOCA encouraged yet more manufacturers to take part in what was fast becoming Europe's leading touring car series. These included Alfa Romeo, Renault and Volvo.

Though it was the old stalwart BMW that provided the winning cars in both that year and 1993, when the ever popular 'Smokin' Jo Winkelhock took the title, 1994 was Alfa Romeo's turn, though not without an element of controversy surrounding the Alfa 155's aerodynamic spoilers. 1994 was also the year that Volvo caused more than a degree of surprise by competing with the first estate car to take to the BTCC grid.

Yet more manufacturers joined the fray in 1995, with Honda in particular making a serious challenge and Volvo, having made its mark with the 850 estate, now switching to the more conventional 850 saloon for the new season. Renault also provided a pointer to

Below: 1988 was Frank Sytner's year as he won the Championship in true style. It was also BMW's first BTCC victory

Right: Gabriele Tarquini was uncatchable in the 1994 season thanks to the advanced aerodynamic package on his Alfa 155

future developments by agreeing a contract with its Formula One partner Williams to run its BTCC programme. Williams duly did the business, because after a hard-fought season with Vauxhall, Volvo and Renault all vying for the title, it was eventually John Cleland in the Vauxhall who took the drivers' title, but Renault who clinched the manufacturers' title.

1996 saw the arrival of the four-wheel drive Audi A4s, which immediately won five of the first eight races. What was perceived to be an unfair advantage conferred by four-wheel drive was counteracted mid-season by a compulsory 30kg weight penalty for the Audis, but it wasn't enough to stop Frank Biela taking the title.

Further weight penalties for the 1997 season prevented the Audis from dominating a second time, and Renault's Laguna, prepared by Williams, was clearly the fastest car of the year. Alain Menu duly took the drivers' title and Renault also took the manufacturers' title by a clear margin.

Today, the BTCC is second only to the Formula 1 World Championship in terms of global prestige and coverage. In fact, TOCA claims that more than a billion people around the world watched the BTCC action during the 1997 season, and the races are shown in no fewer than 120 countries worldwide. For 1998, TOCA reckons it will reach two billion viewers thanks to a new TV contract with mainland China.

The rules and regulations have been tweaked once again for 1998, to ensure that the racing and the spectacle remain as gripping as ever. A new qualifying format involves a One-Shot Showdown session establishing the grid for a short Sprint Race. Then, on the same programme will be a longer Feature Race involving mandatory pit stops to change a pair of wheels and tyres and a revised points scoring system that gives extra points to drivers leading the Feature Race. More details of these and all the 1998 season rule changes are given on page 34.

And just for good measure, there's a special £1 million prize for any driver winning every race. TOCA Chairman Alan Gow says he doesn't expect to have to pay up: 'the racing is just too close and too competitive these days,' he believes.

Above: Renault was BTCC Manufacturer's Champion in 1995 but it was two more years before Alain Menu could clinch the driver's title

Right: Jaguar's heritage is built upon racing and, although Jaguars never won the BTCC outright, they were heady competitors during the 1980s

Below and Left: Perhaps the BTCC's most famous champion was the great Jim Clark, who won in 1964 in a Ford Lotus Cortina. Here in more familiar surroundings, he is seen on his way to Ford's very first F1 victory at Zandvoort in 1967

Right: Volvo caused more than a stir when it decided to go racing with the 850 estate car

Far Right: Touring cars have always offered some of the closest racing and the finest motorsport spectacles

Touring Cars—
The Marketing Story

Motorsport and motor manufacturing have always moved hand in hand. Some manufacturers have used motorsport as a means of boosting the image of their products and of gaining a technological lead on their competitors. Others started life as motor racing concerns and only started building road cars in order to raise the funds necessary to keep competing at the highest levels.

A classic example of the latter is Ferrari, a car company started in the late 1940s by Enzo Ferrari, the man who before the war had been responsible for Alfa Romeo's Grand Prix programme. Ferrari was an out-and-out racing operation and it was only when his race car customers started requesting road-going versions that production Ferraris became a reality.

In later years, although the company remains at the pinnacle of motorsport, being active in Formula One, INSA racing in the USA and also in GT and one-make racing in Europe (the Ferrari 355 Challenge and earlier the Ferrari 348 Challenge), its primary activity is designing and building some of the fastest and most beautiful cars on the road today. And yet the direct link between road and race cars remains, with the latest F550 Maranello being fitted with a detuned version of the F1 engine and benefiting from Ferrari's F1 experience of working with high-tech lightweight materials such as carbon fibre and kevlar.

Ferrari is, of course, a special case. Yet other manufacturers from far humbler beginnings have also successfully used motor racing—and most particularly saloon car racing—as a means of boosting the marque's credentials on the road.

For example, who would believe that a company which effectively started life building motorcycles, small Dixi runabouts and even bubble cars could within a few decades claim to be 'the ultimate driving machine'? And yet that is precisely what BMW have achieved—and as a direct result of its race-track successes.

From quite early days, BMW recognised the value of motorsport in establishing the company's credentials as a significant player in Europe's growing motor industry. A BMW 328 Coupé was the winner of the 1940 Mille Miglia, for example, and although World War II put a stop to racing activities for a while, BMW-powered cars were back on the race-tracks as soon as practicable after hostilities ended. Initially, AFM and Veritas cars, using BMW engines, kept the company in the fray. Later, BMW was to again race its own cars, clocking up a number of notable victories including the 1965 24 Hours of Spa-Francorchamps.

A major turning point for the company came in 1972 when it decided to set up its own in-house motorsports division—BMW Motorsport GmbH, which very quickly made its mark by producing the M17/7 Motorsport-engineered engine that powered BMW to five Formula 2 Championships between 1972 and 1983.

'M-Power' had arrived and it was soon to be shoehorned into a road car—although admittedly an extremely modified one. The CSL Coupé, known as the Batmobile because of its extravagant body styling, took the 1973 European Championship thanks to the 375hp that the M-Sport engineers squeezed out of BMW's straight-six engine and the talents of some of the world's finest drivers, not least of whom was one Nikki Lauda.

Not only was this success working wonders for BMW's image in the showrooms; it was also fostering a demand from the marque's more discerning customers for the

ability to share in the pleasures of M-Power motoring. By 1979 BMW felt justified in investing considerable sums in BMW Motorsport's sites, to allow the company to start limited production of cars.

First to appear was the fabulous BMW M1, a supercar built in very limited numbers but given invaluable publicity because it was used as a one-make support series for the 1979 and 1980 Grand Prix meetings, with all the top F1 drivers taking the wheel in the sort of highly entertaining racing that today's driver contracts would never allow.

However, the first true road car was the BMW M5, externally very similar to the standard 5-Series saloon, but with considerably more power under the bonnet and with suspensions and handling uprated to cope with the added performance. Next up was the M3, which again took the standard 3-Series saloon and turned it into a pocket racer.

Since then, BMW has produced—and continues to produce—M-Power versions of many of its cars, all with the added power, performance and handling that only a motorsport heritage could bring.

Back on the tracks, the Batmobile accounted for every European Touring Car title but one between 1973 and 1979, while the 1980s saw first the BMW 635 Coupé and then the 528i four-door clinch the European Championships, followed by the World Touring Car title and numerous national titles at the end of the decade with the all-conquering M3. The 1990s saw this success continue with the arrival of the 2.0-litre Super Touring series in the UK; BMW Motorsport 3-Series cars won three successive championships from 1991 to 1993 and although there are no longer factory-supported BMWs in the UK Super Touring Championship—perhaps because 'the ultimate driving machine' message has finally got across!—BMW continues to race the M3 in the USA, the company's largest export market.

BMW has been highly successful in linking racetrack performance with road car image. As a result, in the UK and many other markets, BMW has become a highly desirable premium marque, set apart from the volume makers such as Ford and Vauxhall even though very large numbers of BMWs are now being sold. Despite the fact that the vast majority of BMW's sales are of the smaller four-cylinder 1.6 and 1.8-litre Compact and 3-Series cars with relatively undistinguished performance,

Above:
Motorsport provides the whole raison d'être *for Ferrari. Many of its customers actively race their road cars in one-make series such as the 348 Challenge*

the public's image of the brand as a high-powered and sporting marque remains undiminished—and all because BMW Motorsport continues to produce M-powered specials in relatively low numbers, such as the very latest M5 and M Coupé . . .

What a contrast from the image of Volvo just a few short years ago. For 50 years or more, the Swedish car maker had been producing sturdy, sensible and above all safe cars that could cope with the worst the Swedish winters could throw at them, could withstand hitting a moose at high speed—a not uncommon experience on the roads of Scandinavia—and would last for 10, 15, even 20 years of reliable and solid usage.

Volvos were safe, sturdy tanks designed for conservative drivers. They were not cars for those who took pleasure in motoring; they were a practical and sensible means of transport from A to B.

Changing an image such as this, one that

had been built up over many years, was never going to be easy. But at the start of the 1990s, the company decided to gamble on new designs of cars, higher levels of performance and—a first for the Volvo Corporation—an attempt to make the cars fun to drive and therefore to attract a younger, more affluent customer base.

Investments in design and product engineering produced the 850, Volvo's first example of the new way of thinking. Now replaced by the S70 and V70, and joined in the line up first by the S40 and V40 and more recently the C70 Coupé and Convertible, Volvo now has a range that can hold its own with the offerings of most other manufacturers. The cars are still ultra-safe, but they also have a performance and handling edge that never existed before.

This has not come about as a direct result of motorsport experience, but it was success in touring cars that permitted Volvo very quickly to get over the message that here was

Below: Who would have believed that BMW the makers of the humble bubble car could later claim to manufacture the ultimate driving machine?

a new company with new products and a new outlook.

When Volvo decided to enter the BTCC, it did so in a manner that was guaranteed to get it maximum publicity. It reasoned that, since one of the things Volvo was best known for was estate cars, it would race—an estate car!

Volvo chose to go racing in partnership with Tom Walkinshaw Racing (TWR), an operation with vast amounts of touring cars experience. TWR had been competing and winning for literally decades, starting with Ford Capris, then moving to Jaguar saloons, Rover Vitesses and Jaguar XJ-Ss, with which TWR helped Jaguar clinch the European Touring Car Championship in 1984. Later, TWR was to clinch the World Sportscar Championships in 1987, 1988 and 1991 with the Jaguar XJR, and in the same period to pick up both Le Mans 24 Hour and Daytona 24 Hours trophies.

Volvo and TWR entered the BTCC in 1993 with the 850 Estate. The car had little success in terms of podium places, but what Volvo lacked in results was more than compensated by the acres of publicity that the racing estates brought to the company.

The following season, in 1994, drivers Rickard Rydell and Jan Lammers continued to improve the cars, though they still tended to be running in the pack rather than at the front of the field.

However, by 1995 the results started to come—perhaps because by now Volvo and TWR had sensibly switched to racing the 850 saloon. Drivers Rydell and Tim Harvey picked up seven wins during the season and Volvo came third overall in the championship.

1996 saw the last season of 850 racing with more wins clocked up for the sturdy Volvos. The racing 850 cars—both saloons and estates—had done their job of establishing a new image for the Volvo marque, which was no longer associated in people's minds with an odd mixture of retired folk, country-women in headscarves and shady antique dealers.

Above: With its engine based on the Ferrari F1 power unit, the 550 Maranello's racetrack pedigree is second to none

The company's latest road cars provide levels of performance that even a handful of years ago could only have been dreamed about at its Gothenburg headquarters in Sweden.

Without the image change it would have been impossible for Volvo to have launched the tarmac-burning 150mph 850 T5. And even more impossible for it to have been offered in a bright primrose yellow colour guaranteed to attract attention from all quarters. Yet that is precisely what Volvo did, and found itself sitting on orders that would take months to clear, so popular was the idea of a genuinely fast Volvo car.

Since then, the company has launched a series of new and exciting cars, from the V70 and S70 R models, which offer even more performance than the earlier T5. Four-wheel drive models are also now part of the Volvo range, including a unique V70 XC Estate with both four-wheel drive and toughened and raised suspension to permit a degree of off-road ability too.

Volvo continues to race, now with the newer and more aerodynamic S40 model, with which the company has high hopes of lifting its first ever BTCC title.

Interestingly, it seems that at least one other manufacturer has been trying to muscle in on

Below: One of BMW's most significant early victories was in the 1940 Mille Miglia

Volvo's marketing success. Renault, itself no stranger to the chequered flag in many forms of racing, not least in Formula One where its engines have powered successive champions in the 1990s, produced its own racing estate, purely for publicity purposes. Williams, one of Renault's Grand Prix partners, is also responsible for the Renault BTCC programme and it produced the striking Williams Renault Laguna Estate during the 1995 season to publicise the links between the two companies.

Williams' expertise was also put to good use on one of Renault's road cars, the Renault Clio Williams, a hot hatch that Williams engineers had tweaked to make that little bit hotter. So successful was the Clio Williams that although originally Renault said it would only be built in a strictly limited short run, in the event market pressures induced a change of mind and subsequently the Renault Clio Williams 2 and Clio Williams 3 found their way into the showrooms.

Above:
M-Power started life as a purely motorsports unit of BMW but it now also provides engines for the company's hottest road cars

The BMW M1
showed just
how serious
BMW was
about motor-
sport

Right: The BMWs of Frank Sytner and Kelvin Burt leading the field in 1990

Below: The very latest road-going BMW M5, developed in-house by BMW's M-Sports division

Left: Hans Stuck in his BMW 3.0CSL in 1974—the famous Batmobile

Below: Volvo would never have been able to launch a bright yellow 850 T5-R rocket without changing its image via the BTCC

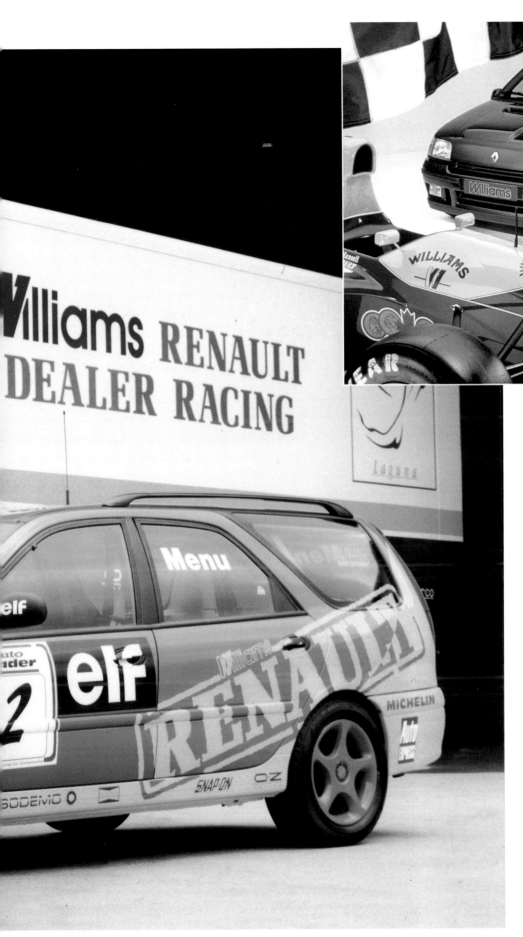

Above: Renault has made the most of its motorsports connections, launching the Clio Williams to widespread acclaim

Left: Perhaps to try to steal some of Volvo's thunder, Renault also produced a racing estate for publicity purposes

The British Touring Car Championship

In terms of global prestige and media exposure, the *Auto Trader* RAC British Touring Car Championship is second only to the Formula One World Championship. In fact, the races which in the UK are shown during the BBC's 'Grandstand' programme, are currently also seen in some 120 different countries around the globe in as far-flung places as Mongolia and French Polynesia.

If this wasn't enough, the championship has also established a significant presence on the fastest-growing media outlet on earth—the world wide web. During the 1997 season, for example, the official BTCC website received no fewer than 2.3 million 'hits'.

The championship's truly international status has encouraged a regular inflow of big-name foreign drivers to compete with the very best of British talent, and this in turn has further increased the interest and attention of the media around the world.

For example, in 1993 it was ex-Formula One driver Jo Winkelhock who took the overall BTCC crown, and the following year it was yet another ex-F1 driver, Gabriele Tarquini, who won the championship in his Alfa Romeo. In 1996 it was the turn of Audi's German ace Frank Biela and in 1997 it was Frenchman Alain Menu who clinched the title.

For the leading motor manufacturers, the BTCC represents an irresistible challenge, which is why so many factory teams are lined up for the 1998 series—more than any equivalent touring car championship. They enter and they compete because the BTCC is wide-ly recognised as the toughest and most competitive touring car series of them all—and that means success in the BTCC carries more marketing weight and kudos than victory in any other championship.

The raw statistics for the 1998 BTCC season are impressive enough: nine manufacturers, five former champions and three ex-F1 drivers.

The very fact that so many car manufacturers are closely involved is a true endorsement of the BTCC's value as a marketing and promotional shop window—as indeed is the length of involvement of some of the manufacturers competing.

The manufacturers recognise above all that the BTCC's high profile can prove a vital tool in pan-market advertising campaigns. 'Volvo is in the BTCC because it is the most international touring car championship,' says Andy King, Marketing and Communications Director of Volvo's racing partner TWR. 'Volvo's BTCC programme is a key marketing resource for every one of its markets around the world.'

Frank Williams, chief of both the Williams Grand Prix team and Renault's BTCC operation, is also in absolutely no doubt as to the value of the series: 'Next to F1, the BTCC is the most important championship in the world outside America,' he says.

Furthermore, it's a mark of the BTCC's pre-eminence in motorsport that attracts Grand Prix-calibre teams. For example, the driving force behind Renault's BTCC success in 1997

BTCC

RAC BRITISH TOURING CAR CHAMPIONSHIP

Above: For the 1998 season, nine manufacturers are competing head to head

and its 1998 title defence is none other than Williams Touring Car Engineering, an offshoot of the Williams F1 team, eight times champion Grand Prix constructor.

Volvo's programme is masterminded by TWR, whose Arrows F1 team put Damon Hill back on the grid in 1977. The BTCC Hondas are prepared by Prodrive, the Banbury-based team behind the Benneton F1 effort and World Rally Championship-winning Subaru.

'The *Auto Trader* RAC British Touring Car Championship—unarguably the world's most prestigious touring car championship—is now entering an exciting new era,' says Alan Gow, Chief Executive of TOCA, the organisers of the BTCC. 'The growing commitment to the championship by manufacturers, independent teams and sponsors alike continues unabated, and for very good reason: no other championship of its type in the world can provide the competition and exposure that the BTCC does. As an example, 1998 will see the global television audience exceed two billion viewers for the first time, nearly double the figures for the previous two years.

'If the BTCC suffers from one thing, it's the title. The word "British" does not truly reflect the fact that this is so much more than a domestic championship. The very best teams and drivers compete in the BTCC and it is seen in every corner of the globe. It is universally recognised as the greatest.'

For the spectators, the BTCC also offers one of the world's greatest motorsport spectacles. Around 30,000 fans turn up for each round—which means the BTCC events draw on average as many spectators as Premier League football games and test match cricket in the UK.

And the *Auto Trader* Championship is unique among major sporting events in that it actively encourages interaction between spectators and their sporting heroes—they are able to see the cars close up, watch the mechanics in action and, most importantly of all, talk to the drivers and get their autographs during the pre-race pitlane walks.

The BTCC is a touring car challenge that has a 40-year heritage supporting it, but which, far from resting on its laurels, gets more competitive and more gripping to watch year on year.

For spectators, BTCC represents ordinary saloon cars driven by ordinary approachable folk in a competitive environment that features both good clean racing along with the occasional little bit of bumping and boring. It's successful as a format because it's approachable, real life motorsport that allows everyone watching to dream that they could be in there, mixing with the best of them.

It's not true of course, because the drivers are a very special breed and there is nothing ordinary about the cars which can best be described as wolves in sheep's clothing. They may look like war-painted versions of their street counterparts but in reality what lurks underneath are genuine 150mph-plus supercars.

Below: Renault wears the No 1 badge but will Alain Menu be able to retain his crown in 1998?

Left: *They may look like fairly ordinary saloons but under the skin they are out and out racers*

Below: *The BTCC provides spills and thrills in the most competitive motorsport arena of them all*

New Regulations for 1998

In recent years, as the major motor manufacturers have invested increasing sums in designing, developing and testing their BTCC cars, the performance of the front-running cars has to a great extent been equalised. In particular, improvements to brakes to boost stopping power and to the suspension to increase grip have tended to make it far harder to overtake. As in Formula One, when the braking distances into corners are reduced, so the opportunity to brake that fraction later and dive down the inside line into the corner is also reduced.

So while BTCC races have never been processional, the organisers TOCA decided that changes to the regulations were required for 1998 in order to maintain the BTCC as one of the world's greatest motorsport spectacles. Motorsport fans at the trackside are joined by a UK audience of more than 50 million during the course of the season, and around the world up to two billion tune in to the BTCC. It's a staggering figure, but the BTCC is now watched on major terrestrial and satellite networks on every continent except Antarctica.

To keep all those viewers on the edge of their seats by encouraging closer and more competitive racing, changes have been made to the BTCC regulations for 1998.

Most important is the introduction of compulsory pit-stops at which at least two wheels and tyres have to be changed. It adds a new element to the racing as now not only do the teams have to carry out the stops quickly and efficiently in order to waste the minimum time in the pits, but also both tactics and teamwork now influence the outcome of the race.

Only five team members are allowed to work directly on the car during the pit stop—two on each wheel and one to operate the onboard air jacking system. One other team member holds the all-important stop board while others will stand watch with fire extinguishers in case of incidents. Unlike Formula One, refuelling during the race is banned. Similar to Formula One, however, strict speed limits will operate in the pit lane. Drivers may not exceed 40mph and are not allowed to use F1-style electronic speed limiters.

Tyre warmers, which up to the 1998 season had been banned in BTCC, are now permitted in the pits and paddock area but not on the grids. Another innovation for the 1998 season is that, at all the venues except Knockhill in Scotland where the pit lane is unsuitable for pit stops, there will be not one but two BTCC events.

The first is a sprint race, rather shorter than is normal in touring cars. The second, longer feature race will be the one in which the pit stops have to take place at some point between 15 and 75% of race distance.

There are new qualifying arrangements for 1998. At each meeting there are two qualifying sessions: the first lasts 30 minutes during which drivers vie for the fastest times to set the grid for the feature race.

The second qualifying session is a One-Shot Showdown at which each driver is allowed just a single timed lap to determine the grid for the shorter sprint race—exactly the same way that qualifying is carried out at the famous Indy 500 race in the USA. What it means is that at each round of the BTCC championship, every driver—even the privateers—have a genuine chance of getting to the front of the grid for the sprint race, by putting in a single faultless lap in qualifying.

And the privateers have an even greater chance of glory this year because for the first time they will all have access to exactly the same tyres as the manufacturer-funded teams use. In the past the independent drivers have been at a serious disadvantage because they were unable to get access to the state-of-the-art tyre technology made available to the works teams. For 1998, this has changed and the result is a more level playing field.

If the independent drivers competing in the BTCC for the TOCA Challenge Cup need any further encouragement, there's a special prize of £100,000 for any privateer who wins a race outright.

As for the works drivers, they also have some serious cash to play for. Any driver winning every race in the season—all 26 of them—will pick up a cool £1,000,000 reward. Win 23 races and pick up £900,000, 21 and it's £800,000, 19 and it's £700,000, which is where the added bounty stops.

Because of the level of competition, it is unlikely that a privateer will pick up that £100,000 prize. And it's even more unlikely that any works driver will win even 70% of the events. But TOCA have taken out insurance just in case . . .

Below:
Because the performance of the top BTCC runners is so similar, overtaking can be tricky, but there is no lack of driver effort

Pit-stops have been intro-duced for the 1998 season to provide added interest to the races and to bring team tactics into play

What's under the skin of a BTCC Car?

Take away the sponsor's stickers and all the cars competing in the *Auto Trader* RAC British Touring Car Championship are instantly recognisable as mass-production 2.0-litre four-door family cars. That's because an important part of the regulations for this series insists that the cars look like their showroom counterparts. In fact, the bodyshell has to be identical in shape and size to the road-going counterpart, and a minimum production run of 25,000 units is essential for homologation.

Under the skin, of course, there are fundamental differences. These are, after all, sophisticated racing cars complying with international FIA Super Touring rules. The engines must be 2.0-litre units—something that virtually every motor manufacturer already has on its production lines—and at least 2,500 production examples have to have been built and sold to prevent richer manufacturers introducing one-off special engines just for the race series. The engine's rev limit is set at a maximum of 8,500rpm to improve reliability and also to try to equalise performance as far as possible to attain closer racing.

Engines of more than six cylinders are banned, and so is turbocharging and supercharging. Unleaded fuel has to be used and catalytic converters are compulsory. In addition, strict noise limits have to be achieved.

The length of the car must be a minimum of 4.2m to ensure that only family saloon-sized models are raced, and a system of minimum weight limits is designed to equalise as far as possible the performance of front-wheel drive and rear-wheel drive entrants. At the start of the 1998 season these were set at 975kg for front-wheel drive cars and 1000kg for rear-wheel drive, though race organisers TOCA reserve the right to make changes in the interests of better racing and more competitive fields. In addition to these minimum car weights a standard driver weight of 80kg is assumed, which means that teams choosing lightweight drivers are forced to carry more ballast.

Again to try to ensure that all body shapes have equal opportunities, restricted front air dams and rear spoilers are permitted.

As far as transmissions are concerned, these have to be mechanically operated and have no more than six speeds. While suspension systems have to be of the same basic type as the road car on which it is based, they are purpose-built and fully adjustable racing versions.

Safety regulations call for immensely strong rollover cages, a double fire extinguisher system, extra-strong driver's seats and six-point safety harnesses. In addition a net is fitted to the driver's window to ensure the head and arms are kept inside the car in the event of an accident.

Those are the basic regulations governing the latest BTCC cars. But they are just the starting point when it comes to the development of a top flight racer—development which boosts the cost of the car from around £15,000 for the showroom model on which it is based, to somewhere between £250,000 and £500,000 for the racetrack version.

The difference in cost only starts to make sense when all the changes are taken into consideration. The starting point is not actually a showroom car but a shell which is modified and strengthened to include a complex roll cage. This not only provides protection for the driver, but also makes the chassis as rigid as a single seater—essential for good handling and to ensure that the minute set-up changes have the required effect. The race-prepared engine—which on its own can cost upwards of £40,000—is usually located lower and further back than normal, to ensure the optimum weight balance for the car. The racing gearbox—usually a state of the art racing six-speed sequential unit—has to be designed to be compact enough to allow for the relocation of the engine; and it also has to be manufactured from lightweight materials to ensure the overall weight of the car is kept as low as possible.

The interior offers little in the way of creature comforts, with the main interior items being a specially-designed driver's seat with a six-point safety harness, a fire extinguisher system and a sophisticated electronic dashboard display. The latter provides vital driver information and is essential despite its daunting £10,000 cost.

The bodywork may look the same as a standard car's but each panel is manufactured from lightweight materials—even the windscreen is specially made with weight reduction in mind. Carbonfibre spoilers at the back and splitters at the front cost a small fortune—and are easily damaged in the hurly-burly of touring car racing—but without them, no matter how skilled the driver, he would be doomed to the back of the grid.

Hand-crafted suspension designs which make the Super Tourer ride closer to the ground and reduce body movement, race brake systems, special shock absorbers, a racing exhaust system and lightweight alloy wheels (as many as 30 rims per car at up to £1,000 apiece are needed for the 12 slick tyres permitted at each meeting plus wet weather tyres) all add to the massive cost of a modern BTCC car.

At the end of the day, quite apart from the difference in cost, there is a radical difference in performance. Around a typical 2.5-mile circuit, it's estimated that the equivalent road car, even after being race prepared, would be some 12 seconds a lap off the pace.

Below:
Touring cars have to use the same body shape as their volume-produced cousins, and also a production-based engine. But there the similarity ends.

Anatomy of a race w

The fiercely contested British Touring Car Championship is widely regarded as the world's premier 'tin top' series. Changes to the BTCC rules for 1998 – the introduction of pit-stops, one-shot qualifying and a new race format – made the opening exchanges something of a journey into the unknown for all competitors.

For the Ray Mallock-prepared Nissan Primera GTs, it has been a fruitful one, returning to winning ways after five years without a victory. The team's successes in the '98 BTCC are not down to luck. The cars are meticulously prepared and on close inspection – in spite of first 'outer' impressions – have a host of 'hidden secrets'.

Very definitely *not* built for comfort, the need of these cars is for speed and precise handling. While the cars are essentially the same as their road-going counterparts, the basic premise is 'if it isn't needed, it isn't in'. So just what is under the skin of a race winner?...

Body talk...

With the sole exception of aeroc the outer body shell must be ide the car's standard road-going ve Aerodynamic 'kits' are restricted tehnical regulations and the pac to work from race one. Once ho no changes to the aero kit are p during the race season

Safety first: cars are fitted with external cut-off devices for use in an emergency

Sitting comfortably?...

The single seat is fitted with a six-point harness and is designed to restrict excesive head and body movement. For extra protection against impact, it is positioned further in-board than on road cars and moved back so that driver sits in line with centre pillar

Further protection is provided not only by the roll cage structure, but also by adding carbon-fibre panels and aluminium honeycomb 'fillers' to door panels

Foot thought...

Feet are 'contained' within a carbon-fibre well designed to restrict lower leg movement in an accident. Pedals themselves are almost vertical – and as in all other areas there are no frills, with unecessary trim removed

Going to

Car's major influence co front splitter have a mini clearance o

Regulations clearance on are slightly le Scrutineers t by letting the tyres – if any touches the g disqualified!

Graphic: Russell Lewis *for Avenue Communications*

Above: Even in race trim, production equivalents of BTCC cars—like these Vectra SuperTouring V6 models at Silverstone—are around 12 seconds a lap off the pace

ner – the Primera GT

Getting the facts...

On-board sensors, similar to those used in F1, record both lateral and 'in-line' G-forces. Data from other crucial areas, including the engine, gearbox, suspension and exhaust is also recorded and downloaded after each run

Angling for success...

To fine-tune car set-up for specific circuits, the camber of each wheel can be adjusted independently, by moving the top mounting, to optimise grip and drive

New rules are the pits...

The newly-introduced pit-stops give teams a whole new challenge. During these mandatory stops – which must be within 15% and 70% of the race distance – two wheels and tyres must be changed.

Cars are raised on four pneumatic air-rams, powered by an external 25-bar air supply, applied through a valve at the rear of the car

Air rams inside car (1)
lower and raise feet (2)

Cool under pressure...

Few things work harder than a race-car's brakes! This results in a colossal heat build-up in discs, calipers and pads. Apart from air forced through the permitted ducting, this is controlled by water-cooling. Via the brake system's small, dedicated radiator and water pump, a 'water jacket' maintains a constant circulation around calipers

Brake specification:
Discs: 380mm x 32mm thick front *(3)*; 280mm x 8mm rear *(4)*. Independent front and rear master cylinders. **Calipers:** 6-piston fronts, 4-piston rears.

Driving force: engine block, head and port spacings must match road car specifications. Beyond this, high-tech racing components abound. Engine runs 30% hotter than road-going version and, along with the gearbox, is serviced after every race

A question of balance...

Of the various adjustments that can be made by the driver 'on-the-run', the most important are the front and rear roll-bar settings. This allows driver to 'shift' the car's balance and grip – via a pair of five-step locking levers in the cockpit – compensating for tyre wear

Windows: all screens are made of the same high-strength plastic that is used in jet-fighter cockpits!

Gearbox: manual, six-speed sequential. Ignition cut-off system allows clutchless gear shifting

Rear wing: restricted to a maximum end profile of 150mm x 150mm and must be contained within overall width of car

Leslie Reid

Tyres: ultra-low profile. A maximum of six tyres may be used per race. Temperatures can exceed 100° in summer races

Wheels: restricted to maximum of 480mm x 230mm. Overall diameter with tyre fitted must not exceed 650mm

...und...
...ynamic ...om the ...h must ...round ...

...ground ...the car ...entific. ...feature ...of two ...the car ...it is

⌐ 80% ──── *Brake work-rate bias* ──── 20% ⌐

The Teams and their Cars
Alfa Romeo

Car: Alfa Romeo 156
Engine: 2.0-litre, four-cylinder in-line 16v
Arrangement: Transverse
Output: 300+bhp
Transmission: Hewland, six-speed
Drive: Front-wheel drive

Suspension: Independent, MacPherson struts front; trailing links and coil springs rear
Tyres: Michelin
Length: 4430mm
Width: 1745mm
Wheelbase: 2592mm

Of all the manufacturers competing in the BTCC, Alfa Romeo has the longest—and perhaps the most glorious—motor racing heritage. The first Alfa Grand Prix car took to the tracks in 1914; in later years the Alfa Corse team was run by none other than Enzo Ferrari himself.

For the British Touring Car Championship, Alfa misses the start of the 1998 season as the team is concentrating on the Italian Championship. Alfa plans a full return to the BTCC in the 1999 season but has promised to liven up a number of British events later in the year by entering its all-new Alfa Romeo 156 as part of the team's preparation for the following year.

In saloon car racing, Alfa traces a winning history right back to the 1960s when the Giulia Sprints regularly took the chequered flag. In the 1970s it was the Alfa GTV that showed the others the way, and in the 1980s the Alfa 75.

A switch to front-wheel drive saw the Alfa 155 take centre stage in 1994 and 1995. During the 1994 season, the 155 was very much the car to beat when Gabriele Tarquini dominated the BTCC and walked away with the title. The Alfa's controversial aerodynamic aids—a front splitter and a rear spoiler—were challenged by rivals Ford after Tarquini had easily won the opening round. Alfa withdrew its cars until the rules were sorted out once and for all, and for the rest of the season the Alfa ran without a rear wing and with the front splitter retracted.

Sadly for Ford and Alfa's other rivals, this did not seem to slow the red cars significantly: in fact, Tarquini later claimed that the revised aerodynamic set up was actually better—though this could, of course, have been gamesmanship. But the fact is that Tarquini had the last word in taking the title by a considerable margin.

The following year was less successful for Alfa Romeo however. Management of the team was passed to UK-based Prodrive (now running Honda's BTCC challenge), but they struggled to compete with the faster Renaults and Vauxhalls because the 155's engine could no longer match the horsepower of its major rivals.

Drivers
For the few races Alfa will contest during the 1998 BTCC season, the drivers are expected to be former F1 ace Nicola Larini and Fabrizio Giovanardi, one of Italy's established touring car aces.

Left: The production Alfa 156 has good looks as well as a fine turn of performance. It was voted Car of the Year for 1998

Below: Alfa Romeo's 156 BTCC entry, expected to debut late in the 1998 season

Above: *One of Alfa's drivers is Nicola Larini, seen here in the earlier 155 V6 TI*

Left: *Though the 156 was originally prepared for the Italian Touring Car Championship, Alfa Romeo has now decided to battle in the UK*

The Teams and their Cars

Audi Sport UK

Car: Audi A4
Engine: 2.0-litre, four-cylinder in-line 16v
Arrangement: Longitudinal
Output: 305bhp
Transmission: Audi sequential, six-speed

Drive: Front-wheel drive
Suspension: Independent, double wishbone front and rear
Tyres: Michelin
Length: 4479mm
Width: 1753mm
Wheelbase: 2610mm

An all-new era for Audi in the BTCC started in 1998 thanks to a worldwide ban on four-wheel drive cars in the FIA's Super Touring category that eliminated Audi's dominant quattro. The Audi A4 quattro had taken Frank Biela to the BTCC crown in 1996 and a string of mighty performances including the runner's-up laurels in 1997, despite weight penalties of 65kg at one time and 95kg at another that were imposed in an attempt to even out the relative performance of the quattros and the rest of the field.

For 1998 Audi has a new front-wheel drive A4 contender, which is not expected to be a front runner initially as the company has a great deal of catching up to do in the field of two-wheel drive technology.

'1998 will be very much a development year for us in the BTCC,' says Audi Sport UK Team Director John Wickham. 'Audi has rallied since the early 1980s and more recently raced four-wheel drive cars. It will obviously take time for us to become fully competitive but it will be a great challenge and offers added motivation. I'm certain it will be a very exciting period for us all and one in which we will ultimately achieve success.'

Since Audi has not raced with a two-wheel drive car since 1981, the team lacks the years of front-wheel drive development that the likes of Renault, Volvo and Honda already have under their belts, but the team remains cautiously optimistic.

'It will take time to repeat the kind of success and domination that Audi enjoyed with the quattro. It will be difficult but I'm positive Audi will get it right,' says John Wickham.

Certainly, Audi are taking the new challenge seriously. It is competing this year in the German, British, Italian and Central Europe Touring Car Championships as well as in the Australian Touring Car series.

The new Audi A4 differs from all the other front-wheel drive competitors in that its engine is mounted longitudinally rather than transversely.

Drivers

John Bintcliffe
32-year old John Bintcliffe first raced in 1992 in the Honda CRX Championship when he won the Honda Driver of the Year Award and was quickly recognised as a rising star

He then switched to Renault Clios and clinched the 1994 Elf Renault Clio UK Cup. The following season he won the Ford Credit Fiesta Championship, a feat that was sufficient to bring him to the notice of Audi Sport UK who gave him the number two Audi A4 quattro drive alongside Frank Biela.

Two second places in 1996 were followed in the 1997 season by two wins in the BTCC and seventh place overall.

Yvan Muller

Yvan Muller's motorsport career started at the age of 15 when he finished runner-up in the 100cc World Junior Kart Championship. More karting successes followed, and then Yvan switched to the French Formula Renault Championship in 1988 when he came third overall, and he came third again in the 1989 French Formula Three Championship.

After two more years in F3 Yvan came to the UK to win the 1992 British F2 Championship before making the logical step up into Formula 3000 in 1993. The same year he took part in the Le Mans 24 Hour race behind the wheel of an Alfa Romeo.

He switched to touring cars in 1994 with BMW in France and was successful the very next year, in 1995, when took the title thanks to nine wins. In 1997 he drove for Audi in the German Super Touring Car Cup and for 1998 the 28-year old embarks on his first UK BTCC season.

Below: The front-wheel drive Audi A4 is driven in 1998 by Yvan Muller (left) and John Bintcliffe (right)

Above: *The road-going Audi A4 was voted Best Compact Executive by Auto Express magazine in 1997*

Left: *The A4 is also busy in Europe, where 1996 BTCC Champion Frank Biela is competing in the German Touring Car Championship*

The Teams and their Cars

Ford Mondeo Racing

Car: Ford Mondeo
Engine: 2.0-litre, V6 24v
Arrangement: Transverse
Output: 300+bhp
Transmission: Hewland, sequential six-speed
Drive: Front wheel-drive

Suspension: Independent, MacPherson strut and wishbone front; Macpherson strut and lateral links rear
Tyres: Michelin
Length: 4556mm
Width: 1745mm
Wheelbase: 2704mm

Ford's outstanding pedigree in motorsport encompasses all the major international championships—F1, Super Touring, World Rallying, CART and NASCAR.

The company has been a leading light in UK touring cars since the 1960s and over the years has clocked up numerous successes with Ford Falcons, Capris, and the Sierra Turbos of the 1980s. More than 200 race wins, two FIA Touring World Cup titles and nine championship titles proves Ford's status over the last 40 years.

The Mondeo V6 first appeared in the *Auto Trader* RAC British Touring Car Championship back in 1993 when it won three races. In 1994 the Mondeo struggled to match the speed of the Alfa Romeos but still managed a handful of victories, and had the satisfaction of winning the end of season FIA Touring World Cup and the Donington TOCA shoot-out.

Though the works team again had a middling season in 1995, with lead driver Paul Radisich finishing sixth overall in the standings, privateer Matt Neal took the Total Cup in his Mondeo.

For 1996 the V6 was moved back in the engine bay to improve weight distribution. though both this and the following 1997 season remained relatively lean by Ford's exacting standards, with the V6 Mondeo drivers failing to make a single podium appearance.

Since then the car has been improved and

evolved and it is now prepared for Ford by West Surrey Racing—the highly successful outfit that has five British Formula Three titles to its credit.

Ford's long-time partner Cosworth has applied its expertise and engineering skills to revising Ford's V6 engine for the latest BTCC Mondeo. Cosworth was originally responsible for developing the V6 for the Mondeo's 1993 debut and continues to work closely with the manufacturer.

For 1998 the Mondeo has redesigned aerodynamics to create lower drag and greater downforce across the car, new brakes and a new cabin layout to make controls such as the cockpit-adjustable anti-roll bars more accessible.

Will it be enough to take Ford back to the top? The company certainly hopes so and it has recruited none other than ex-F1 World Champion Nigel Mansell to compete in a third car at certain events, alongside regular drivers Will Hoy and Craig Beard.

Drivers

Nigel Mansell
Although officially retired, ex-F1 Champion Nigel Mansell just can't keep away from racing and he has agreed to drive one of the Ford Mondeos in certain BTCC rounds this season.

He started his illustrious career by winning eight karting championships, then winning the

1976 Formula Ford Championship at his first attempt, winning 32 out of 42 races. A short time in Formula Three quickly led to his first F1 drive, alongside Mario Andretti in a Lotus-Ford at the 1980 Austrian Grand Prix.

Drives with Lotus, Williams and Ferrari followed and he achieved his greatest ambition—the FIA Formula One World Championship—in 1992. On the other side of the Atlantic, he followed this up by taking the Indycar World Series Championship the following year. Though he retired from full-time motor racing in 1995, his presence in the 1998 BTCC marks a welcome return to the UK racing scene.

Will Hoy

BTCC Champion in 1991 at the wheel of a BMW M3, Will Hoy has been driving touring cars since 1987. His career started in karts while at school; his first full race season was in 1982 when he started in Clubmans Sports, progressed into Thundersports and then on into the British Sports 2000 Championship.

In the 1980s and 1990's Will competed in both national and world sports and touring car championships, including five years in Japan and six visits to the Le Mans 24 Hour race.

1998 is his second year driving the Ford Mondeo V6 in the BTCC. He starts the season already a winner, having clinched the pre-season Silverstone Rallysprint Celebrity TV Challenge.

Craig Beard

Though still only 27, Craig Beard has an enormous amount of experience under his belt including four New Zealand Touring Car Championship titles and two highly successful Bathurth 1000 appearances.

After 10 years in karts, he entered the Formula Ford Championship and took the title in 1988. He went on to win the Formula Atlantic Championship the following year and then switched—highly successfully—to the New Zealand Touring Car Championship. This is his first season in the BTCC.

Below: After being off the pace for a couple of seasons, Ford has high hopes for the 1998 Mondeo V6 24V

Above: Regular drivers Craig Beard (left) and Will Hoy (centre) are joined at three BTCC meetings during the 1998 season by ex-F1 star Nigel Mansell

Right and above far right: The standard Mondeo is one of Europe's best selling cars

Below: The latest BTCC Mondeo has revised aero-dynamics to lower the drag and create more down-force

The Teams and their Cars

Team Honda Sport

Car: Honda Accord
Engine: 2.0-litre, four-cylinder in-line 16v
Arrangement: Transverse
Output: 300+bhp
Transmission: Hewland, sequential six-speed
Drive: Front-wheel drive

Suspension: MacPherson struts and coil springs front; multi-link system at rear with coil springs and adjustable dampers
Tyres: Michelin
Length: 4685mm
Width: 1720mm
Wheelbase: 2720mm

Team Honda Sport is one of the favourites for BTCC glory in 1998, thanks to a well sorted Accord car and some blisteringly fast practice times over the winter testing period.

In three out of the four official BTCC test sessions, the 1998 Honda Accord was fastest of all thanks to a new aerodynamic package, an even more powerful engine and some spirited driving from James Thompson.

Honda's Motorsport Manager, Trevor Elliott, is confident that 1998 will prove to be Honda's year: 'The car has been performing well in testing. We have a different aerodynamic package producing more downforce and the engine is now producing even more power. The prospects all look very encouraging.'

Honda, of course, is no stranger to motorsport, having provided the engines that powered six consecutive Formula One Constructor's Championships for Williams and McLaren between 1986 and 1991.

Honda moved into Touring Cars in 1995 when it entered the British, German and Belgian Championships.

Progress was slow initially, but by the middle of the 1996 season the results were starting to come. The Honda Accord had its first pole position at Silverstone in July of that year, and a maiden victory at the hands of talented

Scottish driver David Leslie at the same meeting. At the end of the 1996 season, Motor Sports Developments (MSD), which had been running the Team Honda Sport operation, handed over to Prodrive, the company which masterminded BMW's late 1980s successes in the BTCC and which also runs Subaru's World Rally Championship winning team. In 1997 the driver line-up was James Thompson and Gabriele Tarquini—who had been BTCC Champion with Alfa Romeo in 1994; both men achieved victories for Honda which took third place in the Manufacturer's Championship.

1998 is Honda's 50th anniversary and the company is hoping to be able to toast not only its first half century as a motor manufacturer, but also its first ever BTCC title.

Drivers

James Thompson
Still only 24, James Thompson is one of BTCC's rising stars. At the age of 14 he started competing in Autotests in a self-prepared Escort before switching to senior karting in 1990 and to cars in 1991, just a few days after his 17th birthday.

In 1992 he was fourth in the Formula

Vauxhall Junior Championship, then the following year he won the National Saloon Car Cup and was selected to drive one of six Castrol Honda Scholarship Civics in which he clocked up an impressive seven wins and nine pole positions from 13 starts.

1994 was his first season in BTCC, driving a Peugeot 405 in the Total Cup for Privateers. In 1995 he came seventh overall in the BTCC in a Vauxhall Cavalier, and became the youngest ever winner when he took the chequered flag at Thruxton that year. Another year with the Vauxhall team in 1996 was followed by a switch to Honda in 1997 when he finished fifth overall, taking seven podium finishes and one outright win.

Peter Kox

Dutchman Peter Kox started his motorsport career in karts in 1978, winning the Dutch title in 1982. Formula Ford 1600 followed in 1983 where he immediately proved his potential by winning the Marlboro Challenge that year and then moving up into FF2000 in 1984.

By 1989 he was driving in the Formula Opel Lotus Championships, winning the European and Benelux titles that year. After two years in the German F3 and British F2 Championships he switched to touring cars, winning the Dutch Touring Car Championship in 1993.

Other significant wins include the Spa 24 Hours in 1995 in a BMW and the Nürburgring 4 Hour race in 1996, driving a McLaren BMW. Last season he partnered Roberto Ravaglia in the FIA GT Series in a McLaren BMW. This 1998 season is his debut season in the BTCC.

Below: The 1998 Honda Accord is expected to be one of the front runners during the 1998 season

Above: The road-going Honda Accord 2.2 has a sophisticaed VTEC engine and is manufactured in the UK

Right: James Thompson is one of the young stars of the BTCC

Left: Dutchman Peter Kox in his first season in BTCC

Below: The Honda Accord Supertouring taking a short cut

The Teams and their Cars

Vodafone Nissan Racing

Car: Nissan Primera GT
Engine: 2.0-litre, four-cylinder in line 16v

Arrangement: Transverse
Output: 300+bhp
Transmission: X-Trac sequential six-speed
Drive: Front-wheel drive

Suspension: Independent, multi-link wishbones front; Macpherson strut and lightweight lower wishbones rear
Tyres: Michelin
Length: 4450mm
Width: 1730mm
Wheelbase: 2610mm

With one BTCC victory already in the bag, Nissan started the 1998 season with high hopes of adding to that tally. The team, which is run by Ray Mallock, himself no mean racer in his time, benefits above all from continuity—the car is an evolution from last year's and the driver line-up is unchanged.

Nissan's return to the BTCC in 1996 was not easy. The team was run by RouseSport, an outfit with a huge amount of touring car experience, but the results did not come and so, at the end of the season, management was switched to Ray Mallock's RML team and the original driver line-up changed to bring in the two Scotsmen David Leslie and Anthony Reid who remain with the team for the 1998 season.

Very much on the pace in the 1997 season, the Primera GT has been honed over the winter months and is expected to provide sterner competition during 1998.

'Considering 1997 was our first full year in the BTCC, we were encouraged by the progress we made during the season and by the end of the year we were challenging the pace-setters,' said Brian Carolin, Marketing Director of Nissan Motor (GB). 'We knew that we could take a big step forward over the winter and everybody working on the programme

has made a super-human effort since then. We know we're headed in the right direction and the initial signs are encouraging.'

The drivers, too, are looking forward to a good season. According to David Leslie, 'The 1998 BTCC Primera is a big step forward in many different ways and the development of the engine has given us a significant increase in power. Also, fundamental geometry changes to the front suspension make the car more responsive, especially in terms of turn-in.'

Anthony Reid said: 'If you're determined to be competitive, as both David Leslie and I are, and overtake people, the margin between being called a hero and a hooligan is still razor thin in BTCC. But with the new race formats, pit-stops and points for leading, the 1998 Championship promises to be a highly entertaining affair.'

Drivers

Anthony Reid
After winning a scholarship at the Jim Russell Racing School, Anthony Reid raced in Formula Ford 1600, FF 2000 and then Formula 3. He then raced a Porsche 962C in the World Sportscar Championship before

moving to Japan where he spent the next five years in Japanese Formula 3 and then Japanese Touring Car Championships.

He returned to Europe as one of Nissan's works drivers in the German Super Touring Cup in 1996 and debuted in BTCC in 1997, driving one of the two Nissan Primera GT cars in which he gained two second places and five top six results. 1998 is his second season with Vodafone Nissan Racing.

David Leslie

44-year old David Leslie has been competing in BTCC since 1991 when he contested a couple of races with BMW. The following year he joined the Ecurie Ecosse Cavalier team, moving to the Mazda Xedos 6 team in 1994 and gaining a works drive in the Honda Accord team for 1995 and 1996 when he notched up three wins. 1998 will be his second season with Vodafone Nissan Racing and he is hoping to improve on his 1997 record of three third places and 10 top six results.

Before joining the BTCC circus, David was a Jaguar test driver working on the XJR15 and XJ220 programmes, and prior to that raced for Aston Martin in the World Sportscar Championship.

Below: Nissan drivers Anthony Reid (left) and David Leslie

Above: Anthony Reid at speed in his second BTCC season

Left: The Nissan Primeras have new suspension for 1998 and should notch up podium places and wins

Below: The road-going Nissan Primera GT, built in Britain despite being a Japanese car

The Teams and their Cars
Esso Ultron Team Peugeot

Car: Peugeot 406
Engine: 2.0-litre, four-cylinder in-line 16v
Arrangement: Transverse
Output: 300bhp
Transmission: X-Trac sequential six-speed
Drive: Front-wheel drive

Suspension: Independent, MacPherson struts front; multi-link independent coil spring rear
Tyres: Michelin
Length: 4555mm
Width: 1764mm
Wheelbase: 2700mm

The Peugeot 406 showed great form in the 1997 German Super Touring series and is expected to start producing results in the BTCC during 1998, especially since Peugeot decided to abandon its in-house works team in 1997 and hand over the racing programme to Motor Sport Developments.

Although it has been competing in the BTCC since 1992, first in the 405M16 and later in the 406 Super Tourer, at the start of the 1998 season Peugeot had still not clocked up its maiden win. This is a situation that Peugeot want to change, for the company has been competing in all sorts of different motorsports events for over 100 years and it is used to winning. In the early 1990s, for example, Peugeot swept the board in the World Sportscar Championship and scored a fabulous 1-2-3 at Le Mans in 1992. Since 1994 the company has been supplying engines for Formula One, first to McLaren and later to Jordan.

Peugeot won the 1991 Esso Saloon Car Championship in the capable hands of Patrick Watts and it was this success that encouraged the marque to graduate to the BTCC in 1992, with a single car entry driven by Robb Gravett.

The current driver line-up of Tim Harvey and Paul Radisich is not lacking in experience and both are more than capable of helping Peugeot to its first BTCC chequered flag.

This is Tim's third season with the Peugeot team, and although Paul is a newcomer to the team for the 1998 season, he has already teamed up successfully with Tim for the 1997 Bathurst 1000 where they had a great race in their Peugeot 406, running with the leaders until the closing chapters of the gruelling race when a mechanical problem on the front suspension stopped them finishing in the top three.

'Looking at test results and the development that has gone into the 1998 car I believe that the Peugeot has a very competitive package and I'm looking forward to winning races in it,' said Paul Radisich. His team-mate Tim Harvey agrees: 'We know that this year's Peugeot 406 has race winning potential and I know there is even more to come from the car. I'm delighted with it.'

Drivers

Tim Harvey
The career of 1992 BTCC Champion Tim Harvey spans 17 years, starting with kart racing back in 1979. After winning the 1981 100cc National Karting Championship, he graduated to single-seater, winning 12 Formula Ford 1600 races in his first season until a bad accident terminated his single seater career.

He switched to the MG Metro Challenge before making the transition to Touring Cars, and winning the 1987 Class A British Touring Car Championship.

He became British Sports Car Champion in 1988, and finished third in class at Le Mans the same year. He also found time to drive a Ford RS500 in the BTCC on his weekends away from sports cars and having got the taste for the BTCC, he made a full-time move to the Championship, driving his Ford to third place in the 1990 series.

He switched to the BMW team in 1991 and won the Championship the following year after a spectacular run of six successive victories in his BMW 318.

He then moved to Renault, helping develop the Renault 19 and then the Laguna in 1993 and 1994 before being persuaded to join Volvo's team in 1995. 1998 will be his third season with Peugeot.

Paul Radisich

One of the world's acclaimed touring car drivers, he enjoyed successive wins in the FIA World Cup in 1993 and 1994 and regular wins in the BTCC since he came to the UK from his native New Zealand in 1993. Prior to that, his motorsport experience was gained down under. Starting in motorcross, he moved to single-seaters at 17 and finished runner-up in both the Formula Atlantic and International Formula Atlantic Series, for which he was awarded the Bruce McLaren Driver of the Year prize in 1983. There followed a number of years in Formula 3 and then a spell in the United States in the Super Vee and Indy Lights championships.

He joined Ford's BTCC team in 1993, finishing third overall that year and the next, and making his mark as one of the regular front runners. He moved to Peugeot for the start of the 1998 season after five years with Ford.

Below: *Radisich kerb-hopping the Peugeot 406 at Thruxton*

Above: The Peugeot 406—one of the most elegant saloons on the road

Right: Tim Harvey, BTCC Champion in 1992

Left: Paul Radisich, who has moved to the Peugeot team after five years with Ford

Below: Peugeot hopes the 406 will show the same form in the BTCC as it has done in the German Touring Car Championship

The Teams and their Cars

Williams Renault

Car: Renault Laguna
Engine: 2.0-litre, four-cylinder in-line 16v
Arrangement: Transverse
Output: 300+bhp
Transmission: Williams sequential six-speed
Drive: Front-wheel drive

Suspension: Independent, MacPherson struts front; trailing arm and torsion bar rear
Tyres: Michelin
Length: 4508mm
Width: 1750mm
Wheelbase: 2670mm

The 1997 season belonged to the Williams Renault team, with drivers' champion Alain Menu winning 12 races and his team-mate Jason Plato taking a further two victories in his debut season in BTCC.

Renault has been competing in the Championship since 1993, when an in-house team prepared Renault 19s for drivers Tim Harvey and Alain Menu. For the following season the new Renault Laguna came on the scene and it immediately proved itself fast, though somewhat unreliable. Two wins and a number of second places brought Renault and Alain Menu the runners-up title that year.

The following year Menu was again runner-up in the driver's title but a total of 10 race victories for the team's driver brought Renault the manufacturer's title.

It was at this stage that Renault chose to raise its game in the BTCC by handing over control of its touring cars programme to Williams Engineering, the Didcot-based outfit that had brought Renault a succession of F1 World Championship titles.

In a sense, this move not only boosted Renault's BTCC effort—and indeed, in the 1996 season Alain Menu was runner-up for a third time in the driver's championship and ran away with the title in 1997—but it also forced all the other teams to rethink their BTCC strategy and raise their own games in order to be able to compete with the new level of professionalism and sheer racing experience that Williams was bringing to the party.

For the 1998 season, Renault's aim is clear: to win again the manufacturer's title and to help Alain Menu become the first man ever to retain a BTCC driver's title since the current 2.0-litre technical regulations were introduced. Perhaps the biggest obstacle will be his team-mate Jason Plato, who impressed many in his first BTCC season with those two wins and a further four pole positions.

There's a new look to the Williams Renault Lagunas for the 1998 season thanks to new sponsorship from Nescafé Blend 37 coffee. This has seen the livery change from the familiar yellow and blue to dark green. But Menu and Plato will be hoping there will be no change to their winning ways.

Drivers

Alain Menu
Now in his sixth straight season with Renault, Alain Menu is one of the established stars of the BTCC having won the championship in 1997 in true style—with 12 wins and a staggering and unprecedented 21 podium places.

He started his career at the Elf Renault Winfield School at Paul Ricard where he finished second overall to Erik Comas, now an F1 star. After two seasons in the French Formula Ford Championship he moved to the UK where he finished second in the highly competitive FF1600 Championship with four wins and 13 podium finishes.

There followed two seasons in Formula 3 and then a switch in 1990 to the British Formula 3000 Championship in which he came second. During the following season he won a BMW driver evaluation test and raced for BMW first in the German DTM and then, in the 1992 season, in the BTCC.

He moved to Renault in 1993 and has remained loyal to the team ever since.

Jason Plato

He started karting at the age of 12, winning the 1982 British Karting Championship (Junior Class) and becoming Junior World Grand Prix Champion in 1983. He remained in karting until 1990 when he experienced his first season in single seaters in the Formula Renault Championship. He was then chosen for the works Van Diemen seat in Formula Renault, and promptly won eight of the 12 rounds and went on to win the European Championship in 1991.

A season in Formula 3 was followed by a season in the British Formula Vauxhall Lotus Championship in 1993.

Jason's first experience of saloon cars came in 1994 when he was test driver for the Janspeed Nissan team, but it was not until he had won the inaugural Elf Renault Sport Spider UK Cup in 1996 with 10 victories in 14 rounds that he got his big break, and the invitation to join the Williams Renault team. Third overall with two victories and nine podium finishes was not a bad start.

Below: The 1998 Renault Laguna—can it emulate the runaway success of the previous year's car?

Above: *Alain Menu studies his road-going Renault Laguna company car*

Right: *1997 BTCC Champion Alain Menu*

Left: Jason Plato has already shown great speed and form despite his youth

Below: A new livery and new sponsors for the Laguna

The Teams and their Cars

Vauxhall Sport

Car: Vauxhall Vectra
Engine: 2.0-litre, four-cylinder in-line 16v
Arrangement: Transverse
Output: 295bhp
Transmission: X-Trac sequential six-speed
Drive: Front-wheel drive

Suspension: Independent, MacPherson struts with light-weight lower wishbone front; multi-link wishbone and trailing arms rear
Tyres: Michelin
Length: 4477mm
Width: 1707mm
Wheelbase: 2640mm

Vauxhall has been one of the stalwarts of the BTCC for many years, with an Astra GTE taking John Cleland to the BTCC title in 1989 and the Cavalier, introduced in 1990, regularly among the front runners. Originally prepared in-house, responsibility for preparing the Cavaliers was entrusted to Ecurie Ecosse, Dave Cook Racing and, later, to Ray Mallock. Finally in 1997, when the new Vectras came along, Vauxhall's BTCC programme was handed over to the Triple Eight racing team.

In 1997, however, the Vectra drivers could do nothing to overcome a poor aerodynamic package which, under the rules of the BTCC, could not be changed once the season had started. In addition, the new Triple Eight team inherited the car late for the 1997 season and had little time for development to catch up the other manufacturers who had been testing all through the winter. As a result Vauxhall had perhaps its poorest showing ever in the championship, trailing all the other manufacturers despite the fact that the Vectra proved itself reliable.

Yet the ingredients for victory are certainly there within the Vauxhall team. The drivers—Cleland and Warwick—have a wealth of experience between them with Cleland one of the sharpest racers on the track and Warwick

hungry for his first BTCC victory. And behind the scenes, Triple Eight has recruited Ian Harrison—the man who earlier masterminded the Williams Renault team—to run the team; and John Gentry, formerly of TWR Volvo, to design the car.

The 1998 Vectra is the first to be wholly built by Triple Eight and it features a new aggressive-looking front spoiler and rear wing to replace last year's design which was developed for the German Touring Car Championship. 'We've taken a big step forward with the Vectra for 1998 and it should be very competitive in this year's BTCC,' said Derek Warwick.

Drivers

Derek Warwick
One of Britain's best-known racing drivers, Derek Warwick's long career includes starting 147 Grands Prix between 1981 and 1993 and winning both the World Sportscar Championship and Le Mans in 1992.

His first motorsport experience was in Stock cars and Superstox, at which he excelled. This encouraged a move to Formula Ford and he won the European Championship in 1976. A move up to Formula 3 saw him become the 1978 Vandervell F3 Champion.

Up again to Formula 2, where he came second in the 1980 European F2 Championship with Toleman. The following year he debuted in Formula One with the Toleman team, remaining with them until 1984 when he moved to Renault. Though he never won a Grand Prix in a long career that also included spells with the Brabham, Arrows, Lotus and Footwork-Mugen teams, Derek was one of the sport's most popular competitors.

He switched to the BTCC in 1985, racing Alfa Romeos, then set up Triple Eight Race Engineering Limited to run Vauxhall Vectras in the 1997 BTCC. This is his second season racing Vectras.

John Cleland

John Cleland manages to combine the responsibilities of running a successful group of car dealerships in the Borders with being a highly successful professional racing driver.

One of the old stalwarts of the BTCC, he has been competing in touring cars since 1989 when his 11 class victories in an Astra GTE won him the overall driver's title. The following year, in the new Vauxhall Cavalier, he was runner-up and over the next five years he continued to race the Cavalier in his aggressive and highly successful driving style, regularly winning races and becoming a familiar face on the podium. 1995 saw him win his second BTCC Championship after taking six wins, five second places and seven third places in his fast and ultra-reliable Cavalier.

All John's racing career has been in Vauxhall products because before the BTCC he raced Thundersaloons, taking the Championship in both 1987 and 1988 in a Vauxhall Senator, and in 1989 in a Carlton.

When Vauxhall changed to Vectras in the BTCC in 1996, John remained loyal to the marque.

Below: After a terrible season in 1997, better things are hoped of the new Vectra

Above: *On the road, the Vauxhall Vectra is the company car driver's favourite*

Right: *Derek Warwick, ex-F1 star searching for his first BTCC win*

Left: *John Cleland, BTCC Champion in 1989 and 1995*

Below: *A new aerodynamic package has improved the 1998 Vauxhall Vectra*

The Teams and their Cars

Volvo S40 Racing

Car: Volvo S40
Engine: 2.0-litre, five-cylinder in-line 16v
Arrangement: Transverse
Output: 300+bhp
Transmission: X-Trac sequential six-speed
Drive: Front-wheel drive

Suspension: Independent, low friction MacPherson struts with coil springs front; multi-link system with coil springs rear
Tyres: Michelin
Length: 4483mm
Width: 1717mm
Wheelbase: 2550mm

Volvo arrived in the BTCC with a bang in 1993 when it scored a massive publicity coup by entering its estate car. Not only did this guarantee Volvo maximum coverage, but it also neatly made the most of the car company's heritage and its pre-eminence in the world of large estate cars. And at the same time it provided them with more car on which to maximise the effect of their's and their sponsor's stickers!

For the first couple of years, the Volvos—prepared by TWR, the outfit run by Tom Walkinshaw that had seen numerous successes in Touring Cars, World Sports Cars and even Formula One—ran in the middle of the field. It was not until 1995 when they switched to the 850 saloon that drivers Tim Harvey and Rickard Rydell started to win races.

For the 1997 season an all-new car based upon the Volvo S40 was readied, and Rickard Rydell, now joined by Kelvin Burt as his teammate, continued to make progress, though perhaps not quickly enough by the standards of previous seasons.

The S40 proved to be very quick and it certainly had significant aerodynamic advantages over the earlier 850 thanks to its narrower and more rounded design, yet the team only man-

aged a single BTCC win in 1997, ending up a disappointing fourth overall.

For 1998 Rydell is joined by Gianni Morbidelli, the former Ferrari, Sauber and Minardi F1 driver who has now decided to enter the BTCC fray. Both drivers are quick and skilled at all-important racecraft.

When Tom Walkinshaw set up the TWR Volvo team in 1993, he set a target of winning the BTCC title within three years. That time has now passed, and with the S40 proving extremely quick in pre-season testing, he and all the team will be hoping that 1998 will be Volvo's year.

Drivers
Rickard Rydell
31-year old Rickard Rydell started his career in karts before switching to the Swedish Formula 3 Championship in which he was runner up in both 1987 and 1988. There then followed five further years in Formula 3, first in the British F3 Championship driving a Reynard with Eddie Jordan Racing, then in Japan with the TOMS Toyota F3 team where he was a consistent front runner, winning numerous races including the FIA World Cup 1992 Macau F3 Grand Prix.

He switched to touring cars in 1994, joining Volvo in the BTCC to race the new 850 Estate. The following year, in 1995, he was third in the BTCC in the 850 saloon, thanks to four race wins and a record 13 pole positions.

In 1996 he again finished third in the championship, having secured four further wins and five pole positions. 1997 with the new S40 car was less successful but Rickard still managed to win one race and make it on to the podium six times.

Gianni Morbidelli

Coming to the BTCC via karts, Formula 3 (he was Italian and European Champion in 1989), European F3000 and then Formula One, Morbidelli's F1 career started with tests for Ferrari in 1989 and 1990 and three races with Dallara-Ford and Minardi-Ford the same year.

For 1991 he continued to race for Minardi while retaining his position as F1 test and reserve driver with Ferrari. He stepped into the Ferrari seat, replacing Alain Prost in Australia that year. After a year with Minardi-Lamborghini, he left F1 for a year in the Italian Touring Car Championship in 1993, but returned to Grands Prix in 1994 with Footwork-Hart, later Arrows and finally a season with Sauber.

The switch to Volvo in the BTCC is a big one for Morbidelli as he has never previously raced a front-wheel drive car. But in pre-season testing at Silverstone the veteran of 65 Grands Prix proved he had not lost his turn of speed—he was second fastest, and finished just ahead of his team-mate Rickard Rydell.

Below:
Morbidelli is on a steep learning curve as he's never raced front-wheel drive cars before

Above: *The Volvo S40 is both quick and nimble on the track*

Right: *Rickard Rydell, who has already proved himself one of the very quickest drivers in the BTCC*

Left: Gianni Morbidelli, yet another ex-F1 star to switch to BTCC racing

Below: The image of Volvo road cars has changed out of all recognition

One-Make Series

Below: One of the great things about motorsport is that there's an opportunity for virtually any sort of car

Saloon car racing in Britain takes all sorts of different forms—from banger racing around greyhound circuits, via various clubman and novice series to different saloon car formulae and right up to the pinnacle of the BTCC itself.

But on the way to the BTCC one of the most active and productive breeding grounds for aspiring drivers is the One-Make Series. The idea is that all drivers compete in near identical cars and so at the end of the day it is sheer driving talent that brings victory, rather than having a more powerful engine or a more sophisticated suspension design. Equally important, unequivocal rules that keep a firm check on modifications mean that the costs of competing are kept within reasonable bounds because drivers are not constantly seeking costly ways of gaining a technical advantage.

Two of the One-Make Series currently being run are actually on the BTCC programme as support races, so spectators can get an early look at the stars of tomorrow.

The Ford Credit Fiesta Championship has for many years provided a fast and furious training ground for young drivers aspiring to move up to the BTCC. For example, current BTCC drivers John Bintcliffe and Matt Neal began their careers in the Ford Fiesta Championship.

The cars are relatively cheap to acquire, and they all have the same engines, tyres and suspensions and so they are relatively inexpensive to run as well. Similar performance means hectic racing on the same circuits that the BTCC circus uses, and what the Fiesta Challenge offers above all is an

education in what doorhandle to doorhandle saloon car racing is all about.

Also on the BTCC programme is the Vauxhall Vectra SRI V6 Challenge, a series that provides great action, close-fought racing and plenty of spectator entertainment.

For the drivers, the Vectra Challenge offers an invaluable carrot—the winner of the championship is guaranteed a touring car drive the following season in the form of the loan of a Vauxhall Vectra Super Touring race car for the 1999 Independents' Cup. The prize is worth more than £100,000.

The cars are all fitted with the same 210bhp V6 engine mated to an F20 six-speed sequential gearbox geared to provide a top speed of 127mph. Since all entrants are supplied with equal cars and equal engines— and the series is 'policed' to ensure the equipment remains equal throughout the season—the series above all allows driver talent to shine through.

Other UK one-make series include the Proton Coupé Cup, which has a total prize fund of £25,000 for the 12-race series. With sealed, tamper-proof engines and identical suspension, wheels and tyres, the formula encourages close and competitive racing without breaking the bank—so it is no surprise that the series has attracted strong support from clubman and novice racers from all over Britain.

Across Europe there are many other one-make series, including the Citroen Saxo Cup and one that even makes room for a racing diesel—the Golf TDI.

Back in Britain, the Rover Cup, based on the Rover 200 saloon, is now defunct and its place has been taken by the MGF Cup—not strictly saloon car racing, but similar, in essence, to other one-make championships because the cars are all equipped with the same engine and tyres so the races are close and hard-fought.

A total prize fund of £90,000 is at stake during the 12-race season with the added bonus that the 1998 champion will also drive off in a brand-new road-going MGF 1.8 VVC.

Above: A breeding ground for new talent—the Ford Fiesta Challenge

Above: All Vectra Challenge drivers aspire to one thing—winning a place in the BTCC

Right: In association with Mobil, you can learn to race in a Vauxhall at Jim Russell's Driving School

Left: The Proton Cup is designed to put the Malaysian marque on the map

Below: Bizarre but true—people race diesels in Germany

Above: The Rover Cup has now been superseded by the new MGF Cup

Left: The Saxo Cup offers low cost racing action in France

The Circuits
Thruxton

Below:
Thruxton Circuit

Right: *Paul Radisich in action at the Hampshire circuit*

Some of the fastest touring cars action of all can be found at Thruxton, a wide open and sweeping airfield circuit near Andover in Hampshire. Best viewing points are at the chicane just before the start/finish straight and at the complex Campbell, Cobb and Seagrave corners in quick succession. The rest of the 2.34-mile circuit is extremely fast, as shown by the lap record which, even in 2.0-litre touring cars, is over 110mph.

Location: Thruxton Circuit, Andover, Hants SP11 8NP
Length: 2.356 miles/3.792km
BTCC record: Peter Kox (BMW 320i) 1m 17.07s, 110.05mph/177.10kmh

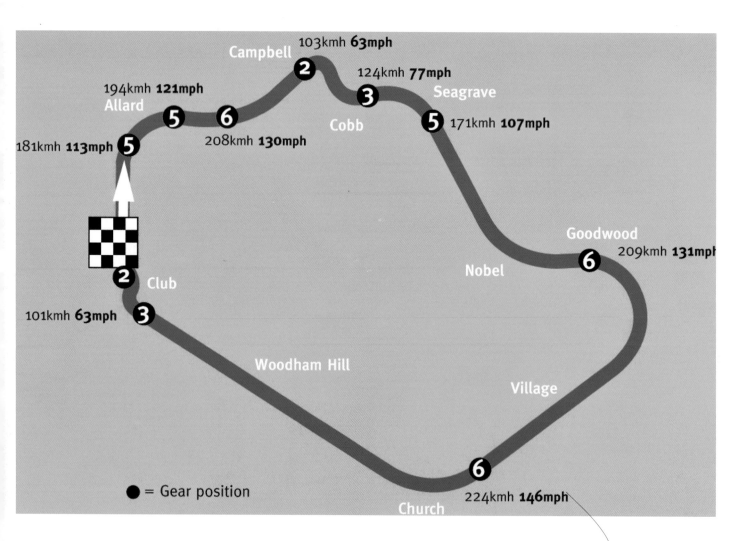

103kmh **63mph**
Campbell
2
124kmh **77mph**
3
Seagrave
194kmh **121mph**
Allard
5   **6**
Cobb
5   171kmh **107mph**
181kmh **113mph** **5**
208kmh **130mph**

Goodwood
6   209kmh **131mph**
Nobel

2
Club
101kmh **63mph** **3**

Woodham Hill

Village

● = Gear position

6
Church   224kmh **146mph**

Silverstone

Perhaps the UK's most famous circuit as it hosts the British Grand Prix each year. Improvements made to the track for the Grand Prix benefit touring cars too, as the new International circuit at Silverstone offers plenty of overtaking opportunities and, therefore, plenty of action. Bridge, Priory, Brooklands and Nuffield corners offer good spectator opportunities, while Maggots and Becketts provide high speed entertainment.

Location: Silverstone Circuit, Silverstone, Towcester, Northants NN12 8TN
Length: 2.268 miles/3.628km
BTCC record: Jason Plato (Renault Laguna) 1m 23.257s, 97.37mph/156.71kmh

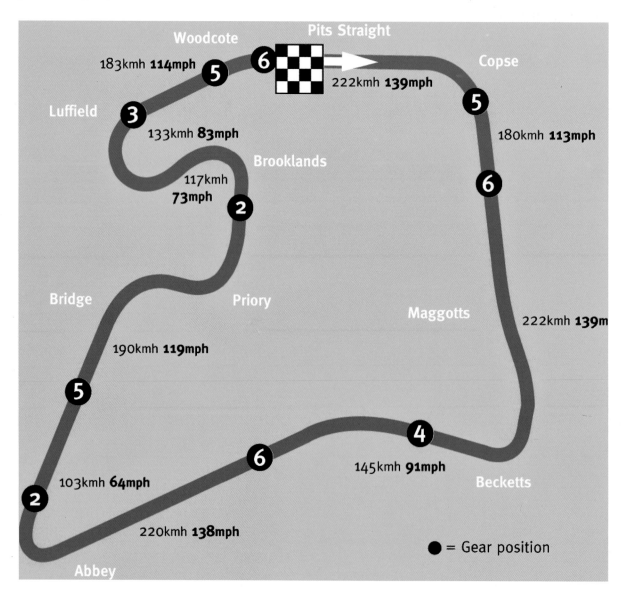

Silverstone Circuit

Pits Straight

Woodcote

183kmh **114mph** 5 · 6 · Copse

222kmh **139mph** · 5

Luffield · 3 · 180kmh **113mph**

133kmh **83mph** · 6

117kmh
73mph · 2 · Brooklands

Bridge · Priory · Maggotts · 222kmh **139m**

190kmh **119mph**

5

4

6 · 145kmh **91mph**

2 · Becketts

103kmh **64mph**

220kmh **138mph**

Abbey

● = Gear position

Donington Park

Below:
Donington Park Circuit

Right: BMW lapping Donington at speed in 1991

One of the best circuits of all from a spectator's point of view and also one of the very best for the drivers, as Donington offers real overtaking opportunities at almost every corner. Most dramatic of all is the downhill sweep of the Craner Curves which are taken almost flat out before the drivers go hard on the brakes for the Old Hairpin—the scene of Nigel Mansell's dramatic accident in 1993. Redgate, at the end of the start/finish straight, is another fine vantage point.

Location: Donington park Circuit, Castle Donington, Derby DE74 2RP
Length: 1.96 miles/3.15km
BTCC record: Gabriele Tarquini (Honda Accord) 1m 11.566s, 98.45mph/158.45kmh

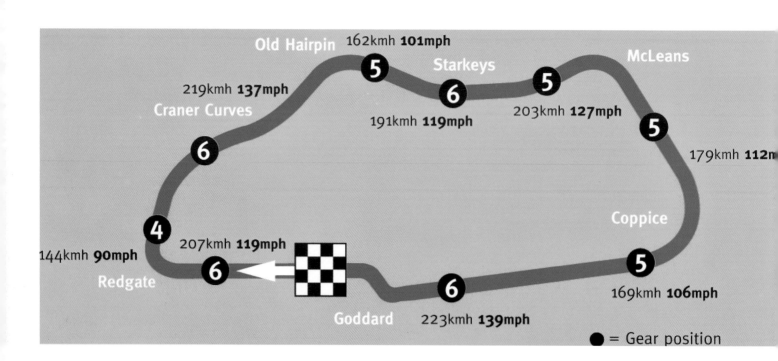

Old Hairpin — 162kmh **101mph**
Starkeys
McLeans
219kmh **137mph**
Craner Curves
191kmh **119mph**
203kmh **127mph**
179kmh **112m**
Coppice
144kmh **90mph**
207kmh **119mph**
Redgate
169kmh **106mph**
Goddard — 223kmh **139mph**
● = Gear position

Brands Hatch

Below: *Brands Hatch Circuit*

Right: *Derek Warwick on the Brands Hatch Indy circuit*

Touring car races take place on the tight and twisting Indy Circuit at Brands Hatch, which virtually guarantees close bumper-to-bumper racing. Perhaps the best place of all to watch the action is on the outside of Paddock Hill, where the drivers crest a brow at the end of the start/finish straight and launch themselves into this fast, downhill corner. Another good vantage point is at the hairpin at Druids, but virtually anywhere around the Brands Indy circuit offers the prospect of touring car action at its best.

Location: Brand Hatch Circuit, Fawkham, Longfield, Kent DA3 8NG
Length: 1.203 miles/1.937km
BTCC record: Anthony Reid (Nissan Primera) 44.674s, 96997 mph/156.09kmh

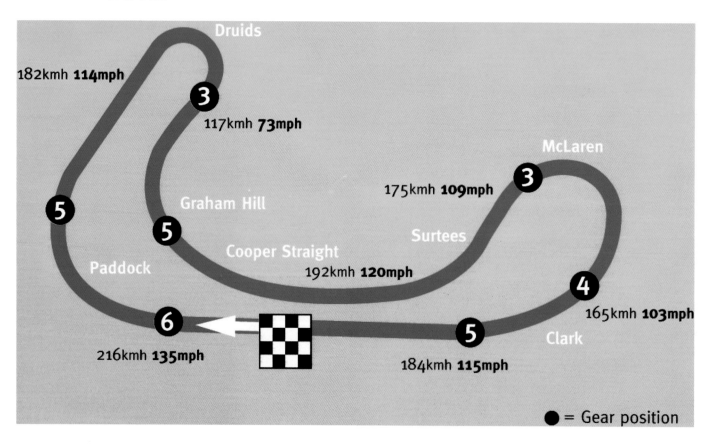

Druids
182kmh **114mph**
3
117kmh **73mph**
McLaren
175kmh **109mph**
3
Graham Hill
Surtees
5
5
Cooper Straight
192kmh **120mph**
4
Paddock
165kmh **103mph**
6
5
Clark
216kmh **135mph**
184kmh **115mph**

● = Gear position

Oulton Park Fosters

Below: Oulton Park Fosters Circuit

Right: Nissan Primera kerb-hopping to shave tenths off a lap time

The Fosters layout at Oulton Park in Cheshire was adopted by the BTCC a couple of years ago and has since been judged a success by both drivers and spectators. Though the layout is rather tight, there is still plenty of overtaking action to be seen here. Best vantage points are Druids and Lodge corners which provide exciting overtaking opportunities as the drivers brake at the end of the straights. Knickerbrook is another good place to watch the action from.

Location: Oulton Park Circuit, Little Budworth, Cheshire CW6 9BW
Length: 1.654 miles/2.66km
BTCC record: Alain Menu (Renault Laguna) 59.615s, 99.88mph/160.74kmh

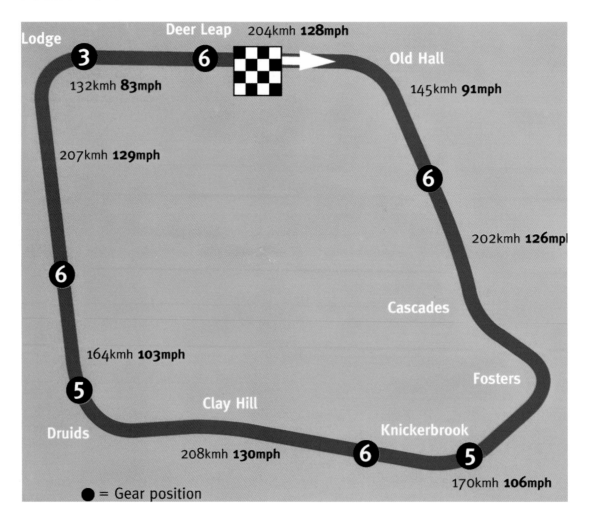

Lodge · Deer Leap · 204kmh **128mph** · Old Hall

3 · **6** · 145kmh **91mph**

132kmh **83mph**

207kmh **129mph**

6

202kmh **126mph**

6

Cascades

164kmh **103mph**

Fosters

5

Clay Hill

Druids · Knickerbrook

208kmh **130mph** · **6** · **5**

170kmh **106mph**

● = Gear position

Croft

The tight and twisting Croft circuit, situated in the North East of England near Darlington, was added to the BTCC programme in 1997 and proved highly popular with the local crowds who came in their thousands to support the series. Tower Bend, at the approach to the start/finish straight, Hawthorne Bend at the end of the same straight and the Jim Clark Esses round the back of the circuit, all offer good viewing potential. Dreadful weather with teeming rain greeted the BTCC's inaugural meeting here last year, so there's added interest in so far as the BTCC lap record is effectively up for grabs.

Location: Croft Circuit, Croft on Tees, Darlington DL2 2PN
Length: 2.127 miles/3.423km
BTCC record: Alain Menu (Renault Laguna) 1m 22.048s, 93.32mph/150.19kmh

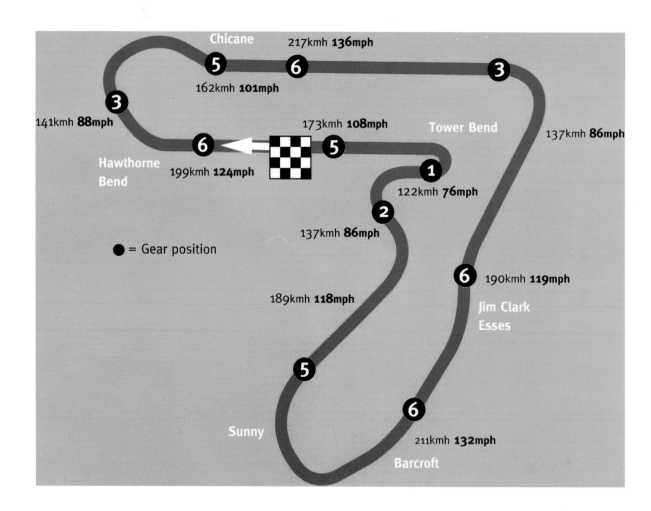

Left: *Croft Circuit*

Above: *John Cleland is one of the canniest BTCC drivers*

Snetterton

Set out in East Anglia, Snetterton is a fast and flat circuit that offers great racing because of all the overtaking opportunities. Best viewing point of all is at the Bomb Hole, taken at high speed by the bravest drivers showing the greatest commitment. The Esses, at the end of the Revett Straight, is always exciting, and there's plenty of action at Riches and Sear too. Facilities at Snetterton can be rather old-fashioned and it can be hideously cold when the wind is coming in from the east, but this is still one of the most important venues on the BTCC calendar.

Location: Snetterton Circuit, Norwich, Norfolk NR16 2JU
Length: 1.952 miles/3.141km
BTCC record: Alain Menu (Renault Laguna) 1m 09.871s, 100.57mph/161.85kmh

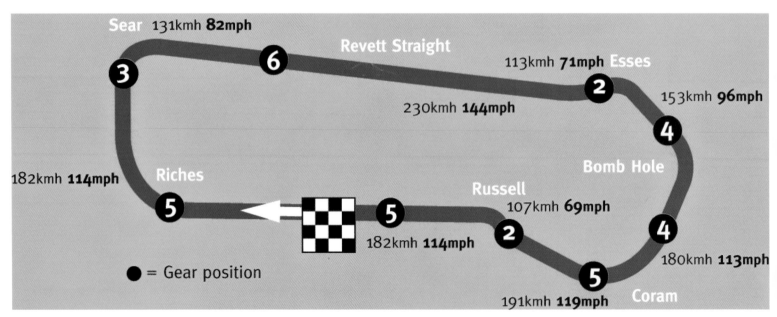

Sear 131kmh **82mph**

Revett Straight

113kmh **71mph** Esses

230kmh **144mph**

153kmh **96mph**

Bomb Hole

182kmh **114mph** Riches

Russell

107kmh **69mph**

182kmh **114mph**

180kmh **113mph**

191kmh **119mph** Coram

● = Gear position

Left: Snetterton Circuit

Above: Paul Radisich showing the way round
Snetterton

Knockhill

The BTCC's annual visit north of the border to Scotland is always an event. The circuit itself is narrow, which makes overtaking difficult, but Knockhill's dramatic swoops and climbs always guarantee excitement and some of the very closest racing—not to mention bumps and nudges. An added element of surprise is provided by the weather at Knockhill which is just north of Dunfermline in Fife—there's always the possibility of a raincloud rolling in off the Scottish hills and drenching the track in next to no time.

Location: Knockhill Racing Circuit, By Dunfermline, Fife KY12 9TF
Length: 1.3 miles/2.09km
BTCC record: Frank Biela (Audi A4) 53.445s, 86.21mph/138.75kmh

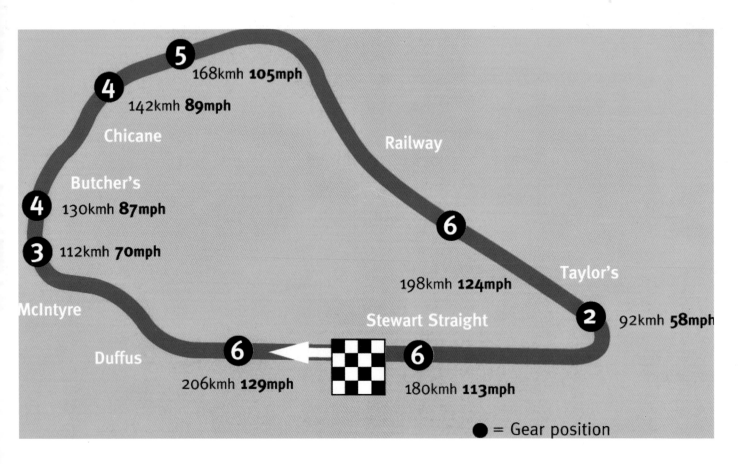

5 — 168kmh **105mph**
4 — 142kmh **89mph**
Chicane
Butcher's
4 — 130kmh **87mph**
3 — 112kmh **70mph**
McIntyre
Duffus
6 — 206kmh **129mph**
Stewart Straight
6 — 180kmh **113mph**
Railway
6
198kmh **124mph**
Taylor's
2 — 92kmh **58mph**

● = Gear position

Left: *Knockhill Circuit*

Above: *Will Hoy at Knockhill in 1997. For 1998 there will be no pit stops because the pit lane is unsuitable*

British Touring Car Champions

1958	Jack Sears	Austin A105
1959	Jeff Uren	Ford Zephyr
1960	Doc Shepherd	Austin A40
1961	John Whitmore	Mini
1962	John Love	Mini Cooper
1963	Jack Sears	Ford Galaxie
1964	Jim Clark	Lotus Cortina
1965	Roy Pierpoint	Ford Mustang
1966	John Fitzpatrick	Ford Anglia
1967	Frank Gardner	Ford Falcon
1968	Frank Gardner	Lotus Cortina/Ford Escort
1969	Alec Poole	Mini Cooper S
1970	Bill McGovern	Sunbeam Imp
1971	Bill McGovern	Sunbeam Imp
1972	Bill McGovern	Sunbeam Imp
1973	Frank Gardner	Chevrolet Camaro
1974	Bernard Unett	Hillman Avenger
1975	Andy Rouse	Triumph Dolomite Sprint
1976	Bernard Unett	Chrysler Avenger GT
1977	Bernard Unett	Chrysler Avenger GT
1978	Richard Longman	Mini 1275GT
1979	Richard Longman	Mini 1275GT
1980	Win Percy	Mazda RX7
1981	Win Percy	Mazda RX7
1982	Win Percy	Toyota Celica
1983	Andy Rouse	Alfa Romeo GTV6
1984	Andy Rouse	Rover Vitesse
1985	Andy Rouse	Ford Sierra Cosworth Turbo
1986	Chris Hodgetts	Toyota Corolla
1987	Chris Hodgetts	Toyota Corolla
1988	Frank Sytner	BMW M3
1989	John Cleland	Vauxhall Astra GTE
1990	Robb Gravett	Ford Sierra Cosworth RS500
1991	Will Hoy	BMW M3
1992	Tim Harvey	BMW 318
1993	Jo Winkelhock	BMW 318
1994	Gabriele Tarquini	Alfa Romeo 155
1995	John Cleland	Vauxhall Cavalier
1996	Frank Biela	Audi A4 quattro
1997	Alain Menu	Renault Laguna